The Colonies

Researching American History

introduced and edited by

Pat Perrin and Arden Bowers

The pilgrims signed the Mayflower Compact aboard the Mayflower *in 1620.*

Discovery Enterprises, Ltd.
Carlisle, Massachusetts

First Edition © Discovery Enterprises, Ltd., Carlisle, MA 2000

ISBN 1-57960-060-3

Library of Congress Catalog Card Number 00-103460

10 9 8 7 6 5 4 3 2 1

Printed in the United States of America

Subject Reference Guide:

Title: *The Colonies*
Series*: Researching American History*
introduced and edited by Pat Perrin and Arden Bowers

Nonfiction
Analyzing documents re: Colonial America

Credits:

Cover illustration: Detail from "Roger Williams being welcomed by the Narragansett Indians," courtesy of the New York Public Library.

Other illustrations: Credited where they appear in the book.

Special Thanks

To the students (school year 1999-2000) of
Andrea Weisman, Yarmouth, Maine, for their help
in reviewing the layout and text for this book.

Contents

About the Series

Researching American History is a series of books which introduces various topics and periods in our nation's history through the study of primary source documents.

Reading the Historical Documents

On the following pages you'll find words written by people during or soon after the time of the events. This is firsthand information about what life was like back then. Illustrations are also created to record history. These historical documents are called **primary source materials**.

At first, some things written in earlier times may seem hard to understand. Language changes over the years, and the objects and activities described might be unfamiliar. Also, spellings were sometimes different. Below is a model which describes how we help with these challenges.

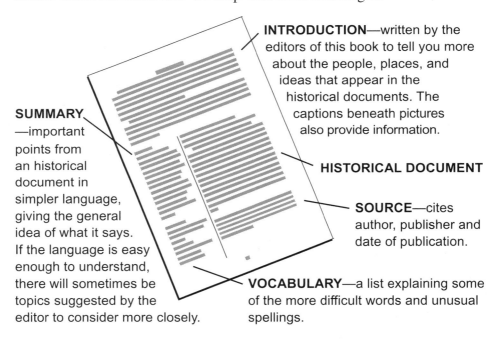

INTRODUCTION—written by the editors of this book to tell you more about the people, places, and ideas that appear in the historical documents. The captions beneath pictures also provide information.

SUMMARY—important points from an historical document in simpler language, giving the general idea of what it says. If the language is easy enough to understand, there will sometimes be topics suggested by the editor to consider more closely.

HISTORICAL DOCUMENT

SOURCE—cites author, publisher and date of publication.

VOCABULARY—a list explaining some of the more difficult words and unusual spellings.

In these historical documents, you may see three periods (…) called an ellipsis. It means that the editor has left out some words or sentences. You may see some words in brackets, such as [and]. These are words the editor has added to make the meaning clearer. When you use a document in a paper you're writing, you should include any ellipses and brackets it contains, just as you see them here. Be sure to give complete information about the author, title, and publisher of anything that was written by someone other than you.

Introduction:
The American Colonies

by
Pat Perrin

In this book, you will find information about the first English-speaking communities in America, called the American Colonies. Included are many words written by the colonists themselves.

A **colony** is a group of people who have left their own country to live in another land, often far away from their original home. The territory they settle is also called a colony. It is still ruled by the country the people came from.

Those who live in a colony are called **colonists**. To **colonize** means to form a new colony.

Colonial means a time or place when there were colonies—Colonial America, for example. "Colonial" can also describe things made in the colonies or anything that looks similar, such as a colonial style house.

Colonialism is the practice of setting up new colonies in other lands. Sometimes "colonialism" is used to mean a country's desire to control the people of a less powerful country.

Long before the United States existed, people from several European countries, Spain especially, explored North America. Since it was new to the Europeans, they called it the New World. Late in the sixteenth century (the late 1500s) the English were interested in owning more territory. The settlers they sent to the New World colonized the east coast of what is now the United States.

In 1607, the first permanent English colony was set up at Jamestown. In 1620, English Puritans settled the Plymouth Colony in New England. Other colonists followed, including many who were not English. Thousands of Africans were also brought to the colonies as slaves.

The colonists brought very different ideas about religion with them. They also often disagreed about the best kind of government to have.

Of course, the New World was not new to everyone. Native Americans were called Indians by the colonists. Sometimes the newcomers and the Indians got along well. Sometimes they fought bitter wars.

The American colonial period lasted about 170 years. After the Revolutionary War in 1776, the 13 American colonies became the first 13 American states.

NovⱯ BritⱯnniⱯ.
OFFERING MOST
Excellent fruites by Planting in
Virginia.

Exciting all such as be well affected
to further the same.

Lⱺndⱺn
Printed for Samⱱeⱡ Macham, and are to be sold at
his Shop in Pauls Church-yard, at the
Signe of the Bul-head.
1 6 0 9.

*In order to attract more settlers, the colonists
sometimes placed ads in English publications.*
(Courtesy of the National Archives)

Those who wanted to settle in the New World traveled across the Atlantic Ocean in ships like the one pictured above. The trip could take as long as four months and, unfortunately, some people did not live to reach America. Many of those who did arrive in the colonies were often weak and hungry. They weren't ready to face the hardships that lay ahead.

The famous *Mayflower,* a ship similar to the one pictured, set sail in 1620 with 102 colonists. Nine weeks later, the pilgrims landed at Cape Cod. They endured many hardships in order to found a free community.

Surviving in a New World

People left their homes in the old world with high hopes for a better life in a new land. Some left to escape poverty. Many wanted to be free to live however they wished. Because they didn't know how to live in the wilderness, the settlers faced many problems in the New World.

The earliest colonists arrived at Roanoke Island in 1584. Some stayed on the island while a ship returned to England for more supplies. When the ship returned three years later, all the colonists had disappeared.

Jamestown was settled in 1608, but that colony just barely survived. Finally, new settlers joined them, and they learned how to live more safely and comfortably.

Making the Trip

Thomas Newe traveled to the New World some years after the pilgrims arrived on the *Mayflower*. He made the trip to Charles Town in the Carolina colony in the 1680s. Even then, the voyage was very hard. After his arrival, Newe wrote to his father about it.

[On the voyage from England] I had my health very well except a day or two of Sea sickness but most of the other passengers were much troubled with the scurvy; Of 62 that came out of England we lost 3, two of them were seamen, one dyed of the scurvey, the other fell overboard, the third was a woman in child bed, her child died shortly after her....

Source: *Chronology and Documentary Handbook of the State of South Carolina.* Dobbs Ferry, NY: Oceana Publications, 1978, pp. 83-4.

Summary:
I stayed healthy except for a day or two of sea sickness. Most other passengers had trouble with scurvy. Of 62 people who came from England, three died. One seaman died of scurvy; another fell overboard. A woman died in childbirth, and her child soon died too.

Vocabulary:
dyed = died
poverty = being poor
scurvey (scurvy) = a
   disease caused by lack
   of vitamin C

Early Settlers

Early settlers usually were not trained builders. They didn't even have good tools. They built huts out of chunks of grass, dirt, matted roots, and anything else they could find. Some burrowed into hillsides. They soon began to send messages back to England, asking for skilled workmen—with decent tools—to join their settlement. Within a few years, the colonists were putting up better buildings.

John Smith was an English soldier who came to America in 1607. He was president of the Jamestown colony in 1608 and 1609. He was known for his interest in trading with the Indians and his love of hard work. Later, he returned to England and wrote many stories about English colonists in America.

Summary:

When I first came to Virginia, I remember we hung a covering from the trees to protect us from the sun. We moved to an old rotten tent when it rained. This was our Church until we built an ugly building like a barn. Later, our first rough houses still did not protect us from the bad weather.

Vocabulary:

awning = canvas covering
curiosity = strangeness
foul = bad
homely = ugly
of the like = the same as
planks = boards
unhewed = uncut

When I first went to Virginia, I well remember we did hang an awning to three or four trees to shadow us from the sun; our walls were rails of wood, our seats unhewed trees til we cut planks, our Pulpit a bar of wood nailed to two neighboring trees. In foul weather we shifted into an old rotten tent; for we had no better.... This was our Church, til we built a homely thing like a barn.... The best of our houses [were] of the like curiosity but for the most part far worse workmanship, that could neither well defend [from] wind nor rain.

Source: John Smith, *Advertisements for the Unexperienced Planters of New England, or Anywhere*, London, 1631. Found in James Marston Fitch, *American Building: The Forces That Shape It*, Boston: Houghton Mifflin, 1948, pp. 2-3.

Cavalier   Puritan   Hollander   Quaker

The 13 original colonies were settled by people from many different European countries, including England, France, Holland, Germany, and Scotland. Some were poor and others were rich. People of different religions, such as Puritans and Quakers, came to America to make a new life.

"Gentleman" Settlers

Many early settlers were "gentlemen," used to a life of ease. Not enough workmen came who could build good shelters or find food. English poet Michel Drayton described Virginia as "Earth's only paradise," even though more than half of the early colonists died young.

Colonist James Percy reported many of the hardships in Jamestown.

Our men were destroyed with cruell diseases, as Swellings…Burning Fevers, and by wars; and some departed suddenly; but for the most part *they died of meere famine!* There were never Englishmen left in a foreigne Country in such miserie as wee were in this newly discovered Virginia.

Source: Mrs. Roger A. [Sara] Pryor, *The Birth of the Nation.* New York: Grossett & Dunlap, 1907, pp. 104-105.

Summary:
Terrible diseases and wars killed many, but even more starved to death.

Vocabulary:
cruell (cruel) = unkind
famine = lack of food
foreigne (foreign) = unknown
meere (mere) = simple
miserie = misery
Swellings = boils or infections
wee = we

A detail from The Peaceable Kingdom, *painted by Edward Hicks in 1846. The New World was beautiful, strange, and frightening to many settlers. Edward Hicks envisioned a peaceful land, with helpful Indians and friendly animals. He painted over 100 versions of the same subject.*

Meeting Native Americans

Of course, people were already living in the land reached by the colonists. These Native Americans were comfortable and safe in their well-built huts and tipis made of animal skins. They made their way through the forests and swamps with ease. And Indians knew how to kill animals for clothes, shelter, and food, as well as how to grow crops.

A Native American named Squanto was captured by a colonist in 1614 and taken to Spain as a slave. He also lived in England for a while. He was later returned to America and brought to Plymouth colony, where the pilgrims from the *Mayflower* had settled. By that time, Squanto spoke English well enough to be of great help to the colonists.

William Bradford was governor of Plymouth colony for 30 years, beginning in 1621. He was a strong, steady leader, and he helped to keep his people healthy and safe. His journal, *Of Plymouth Plantation*, is one of the best sources of the pilgrims' experiences.

All this while the Indians came skulking about them, and would sometimes show themselves aloof off, but when any approached near them, they would run away; and once they stole away their tools where they had been at work and were gone to dinner. But about the 16th of March, a certain Indian came boldly amongst them and spoke to them in broken English, which they could well understand, but marveled at it. At length they understood by discourse with him, that he was not of these parts, but belonged to the eastern parts where some English ships came to fish, with whom he was acquainted and could name sundry of them by their names, amongst whom he had got his language. He became profitable to them in acquainting them with many things concerning the state of the country in the east parts where he lived, which was afterwards profitable unto them; as also of the people here, of their names, number and strength, of their situation and distance from this place, and who was chief amongst them. His name was Samoset. He told them also of another Indian whose name was Squanto, a native of this place, who had been in England and could speak better English than himself.

Being, after some time of entertainment and gifts dismissed, a while after he came again, and five more with him, and they brought again all the tools that were stolen away before, and made way for the coming of their great Sachem, called Massasoit. Who, about four or five days after, came with the chief of his friends and other attendance, with the aforesaid Squanto. With whom, after friendly entertainment and

(continued on next page)

Summary:

At first, the Indians kept their distance, and once they stole some tools.

In March, an Indian came bravely into the settlement. He spoke some English, which he had learned from men on ships.

This Indian, named Samoset, taught the settlers about the new country and about his own people. He said another Indian, named Squanto, spoke better English.

After he was entertained and given gifts, Samoset left and returned with the tools. He said the great chief, Massasoit, was coming to visit the settlers.

Vocabulary:
acquainting = introducing
aloof = away
amongst = among
discourse = conversation
sachem = chief
skulking = sneaking about
sundry = various
was acquainted = knew

Summary:

Samoset returned with Massasoit and Squanto. The settlers and Indians made peace. They agreed that Indians would do the settlers no harm, and any Indian that did so would be sent to the settlers to be punished.

Each side would help the other in any unjust war. Massasoit would let his neighbors know of the agreement. And Indians would leave their bows and arrows behind when they visited.

The chiefs left, but Squanto stayed with the settlers as their helper. He taught them how to plant corn and to fish, and how to get other things they needed. He guided them through unfamiliar places and never left them.

Vocabulary:

certify = notify officially
commodities = products
comprised = included
confederates = friends
hath = has
interpreter = translator
procure = obtain

some gifts given him, they made a peace with him (which hath now continued this 24 years) in these terms:

1. That neither he nor any of his should injure or do hurt to any of their people.

2. That if any of his did hurt to any of theirs, he should send the offender, that they might punish him.

3. That if anything were taken away from any of theirs, he should cause it to be restored; and they should do the like to his.

4. If any did unjustly war against him, they would aid him; if any did war against them, he should aid them.

5. He should send to his neighbours confederates to certify them of this, that they might not wrong them, but might be likewise comprised in the conditions of peace.

6. That when their men came to them, they should leave their bows and arrows behind them.

After these things he returned to his place called Sowams, some 40 miles from this place, but Squanto continued with them and was their interpreter and was a special instrument sent of God for their good beyond their expectation. He directed them how to set their corn, where to take fish, and to procure other commodities, and was also their pilot to bring them to unknown places for their profit, and never left them till he died.

Source: William Bradford, *Of Plymouth Plantation,* New York, Alfred A. Knopf, 1966.

The First Thanksgiving

Today, Americans tend to think about the Pilgrims each year at Thanksgiving. We picture them having a grand feast with their Indian friends. And it is true that they did have such a feast. They also thanked God for the harvest, and for their health. However, that first Thanksgiving might have been less important to them than to us. Governor Bradford mentioned it in only one paragraph in his history of the Plymouth colony.

They began now to gather in the small harvest they had, and to fit up their houses and dwellings against winter, being all well recovered in health and strength and had all things in good plenty. For as some were thus employed in affairs abroad, others were exercised in fishing, about cod and bass and other fish, of which they took good store, of which every family had their portion. All the summer there was no want; and now began to come in store of fowl, as winter approached, of which this place did abound when they came first (but afterward decreased by degrees). And besides waterfowl there was great store of wild turkeys, of which they took many, besides venison, etc. Besides they had about a peck a meal a week to a person, or now since harvest, Indian corn to that proportion. Which made many afterwards write so largely of their plenty here to their friends in England, which were not feigned but true reports....

Source: William Bradford, *Of Plymouth Plantation,* New York, Alfred A. Knopf, 1966.

Summary:

They gathered the harvest and fixed up their houses for winter. All were in good health and had plenty. Since some worked at business, others fished. Every family shared. There were fewer birds here than when the settlers first came. But they had waterfowl, wild turkeys, deer meat and other meat. They had enough corn meal or Indian corn for each person. Many wrote to friends in England about the plenty here, which was true.

Vocabulary:

degrees = little by little
did abound = was full of
dwellings = places to live, homes
exercised = put to work
feigned = put-on/pretended
fowl = game birds
largely = a lot
peck = 8 quarts
thus = in this way

Anonymous drawing of the Boston harbor, showing tradesmen at work. In the harbor, British ships keep watch over the colonies.

Community Life

The Northern villages were small and spread out along rivers and bays near the coast. The center of each town usually had a meetinghouse (also the church), a schoolhouse, and a jail. Small private houses with barns and outhouses (bathrooms) were nearby. Behind each house was a stretch of land for farming. Woods in the area provided wood for building and for burning in fireplaces. Larger farms spread out over several miles from each town.

Southerners had much larger farms (called plantations) where tobacco, grain, rice, and indigo (a dye plant) were most usually grown. Towns were not as common in the South. Plantations and large estates provided everything needed for those who lived there.

Colonists worked their farms and led solitary lives for the most part. Churches were the main centers of social life in the early days.

Detail from The Roberts view of Charles Town, *1739. Charles Town (called Charleston today) was settled in 1670, and named after Charles II, king of England. Since the city sat on a bay leading to the Atlantic Ocean, it became a major trading center for slaves, rice, indigo, and cotton.* (Courtesy of the New York Public Library)

New Cities and Towns

All the colonial villages began with a small group of houses. Soon, a town center would contain a meetinghouse (which also served as a church), a school house, a stockade (jail), and a store that sold household goods. Usually a tavern (bar) would follow, where people could have a drink, conduct business, or bank their money.

Some settlements grew very fast: especially those that were located on a large river or sea. Towns such as Boston and Charles Town became shipping centers for bringing in goods from Europe.

Thomas Newe arrived in Carolina in the 1680s. (See page 7 of this book to read about his sea voyage). His letters to his father also described his life in Charles Town.

Summary:

This town has grown from three or four houses to about 100 wooden houses. The food here is expensive, but better than English food. Some men sell a lot of cattle to new people, but no one likes to kill them and that is why beef costs so much. The people living in the country get deer meat, fish and birds from the Indians for a very small price. The butter and cheese is as good as in England. The grape vines are not yet mature enough to produce wine.

Vocabulary:

beefe = beef
Countrey = country
dear = expensive
flourish = grow
mault = beer
Molossus = molasses
Severall = several
trifles = small amounts
tho = though
tryall = trial
whilst = while

The Town which two years since had but 3 or 4 houses, hath now about a hundred houses in it, all which are wholly built of wood, tho here is excellent Brick made, but little of it. All things are very dear in the Town; milk 2 [pence] a quart, beefe 4 [pence] a pound, pork 3 [pence], but far better then our English, the common drink of the Countrey is Molossus and water, I don't hear of any mault that is made hear [here] as yet. Severall in the Country have great stocks of Cattle and they sell so well to new comers that they care not for killing, which is the reason provision is so dear in the town, whilst they in the Country are furnisht with Venison, fish, and fowle by the Indians for trifles, and they that understand it make as good butter and cheese as most in England....[If] they can make good wine [here], which they have great hopes of, and this year will be the time of tryall which if it hits no doubt but the place will flourish exceedingly, but if the vines do not prosper I question whether it will ever be any great place of trade.

Source: *Chronology and Documentary Handbook of the State of South Carolina.* Dobbs Ferry, NY: Oceana Publications, 1978, pp. 83-4.

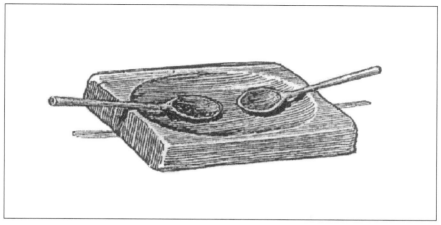

A colonial trencher, used at family meals. A trencher was made from a square block of wood, three or four inches thick. The block was scooped out in the middle to make a space for food. Often, at least two people ate from one trencher.

Family Life

Families lived in small wooden houses. They gathered in the kitchen where the wood fire kept them warm. The fire also heated a built-in oven used for cooking meals.

The children, servants, and women told stories, knitted stockings, and prepared food. Water was carried in from a spring and heated over the fire. When the family sat down to eat, children were sometimes not allowed to sit. They stood behind their parents, who handed them food.

Since so many people died from disease, childbirth, or general hardship, the colonists often married three or four times. As a result, families often included step children and step parents. The families were also large because each woman usually had many children.

By the time they were five years old, children helped with the chores. The girls learned to knit and help prepare food, and the boys helped chop wood, hunt, and take care of the crops. There was little time for play. Everyone, including children, worked very hard all the time just to stay fed, warm, and safe.

Church was an important part of the life for colonial families, and attendance was usually required. To the adults, at least, attending church was also a recreation.

William Byrd was born in Virginia, but went to school in England. He was an important leader in the Virginia colony. His mansion had the colony's largest library. His diaries tell about the lives and values of some of Virginia's wealthy and powerful families in the early 1700s.

Summary:

I got up at 5 o'clock, read, said prayers, and did exercises. Two servants were beaten. I read in the afternoon and had tough chicken for dinner. I walked around the plantation and said my evening prayers.... I told Anaka she would be beaten if she didn't tell about a secret affair. She talked and wasn't beaten. My wife was angry for no reason. I tried to please her, knowing that women have weak minds. I rose before 6 o'clock...My wife and I made each other angry.

Vocabulary:

confess = tell
consideration = concern
contrary = opposite
endeavored = tried
intrigue = secret affair
plantation = large farm
prevented = stopped
reproached = blamed
whipped = beaten

I rose at 5 o'clock this morning and read a chapter in Hebrew and 200 verses in Homer's Odyssey. I ate milk for breakfast. I said my prayers. Jenny and Eugene [servants] were whipped. I danced my dance [gymnastic exercises]. I read law in the morning and Italian in the afternoon. I ate tough chicken for dinner. In the evening I walked about the plantation. I said my prayers. I had good thoughts, good health, and good humor this day, thanks be to God Almighty.... I threatened Anaka [servant] with a whipping if she did not confess the intrigue between Daniel and Nurse, but she prevented by a confession. My wife was out of humor for nothing. However, I endeavored to please her again, having consideration for a woman's weakness. I rose before 6 o'clock...I reproached my wife with ordering the old beef to be kept and the fresh beef to be used first, contrary to good management, on which she was pleased to be very angry and this put me out of humor.

(continued on next page)

I went away presently after dinner to look after my people…when I returned…my wife came and begged my pardon and we were friends again.… My wife and I had another foolish quarrel about my saying she listened at the top of the stairs, which I suspected, in jest. However, I bore it with patience and she came soon after and begged my pardon.… I settled my accounts and read some Dutch.… Anaka was whipped yesterday for stealing the rum and filling the bottle up with water. I said my prayers and ate chocolate for breakfast. I heard guns this morning, by which we understood that the fleet was come in.… [I] sent my boat for my letters. In the evening the boat…brought some letters for me from England, with an invoice of things sent for by my wife which are enough to make a man mad. It put me out of humor very much. I neglected to say my prayers, for which God forgive me.… I had like to have whipped my maid Anaka for her laziness but I forgave her. I read a little geometry.… In the afternoon I played at piquet with my own wife and made her out of humor by cheating her.… In the afternoon I beat Jenny for throwing water on the couch.

Source: Noel Rae, ed., *Witnessing America*. New York: Penguin Books, 1996, p. 139.

Summary:
I left after dinner to care for my workers and when I returned, my wife said she was sorry.… My wife and I argued again, but I was patient and she apologized.… I paid my bills and read some Dutch.… Anaka was beaten yesterday for stealing the rum. This morning we heard guns, which told us the boats from England were here. I got mail and a bill for items my wife had ordered from England, which made me angry. I wanted to beat Anaka for being lazy, but I forgave her. I read a little mathematics.… I played cards with my wife and made her angry by cheating.… I beat Jenny for throwing water on the couch.

Vocabulary:
fleet = group of ships
invoice = bill
jest = joke
piquet = card game
quarrel = fight
rum = alcoholic drink

Early spelling book used in Colonial schools. In 1783 Noah Webster issued the first American Spelling Book.

Schools and Teachers

Many teachers in the colonies were not well educated. In the South, schools were rare since plantation owners hired private tutors, and the other farms were too far apart to have a "neighborhood" school. Sometimes they could manage a "field school" if a group of farms were close enough together.

John Harrower, a servant in Virginia, worked as a teacher to earn money to bring his family to America. From 1773 to 1776, he wrote letters to his wife and children in London, describing his life in the colonies. Harrower's spelling and grammar were not very good; he probably had little schooling himself.

I am now settled with on[e] Colonel Wm. Daingerfield Esqr of Belvidera.... My business is to teach his Children to reaad write and figure. Edwin his oldest son about 8 years of [age] Bathurest his second 6 years of age and William his youngest son 4 years of age. He has also a Daugher whose name is Hanna Basset. ...I am...obliged to talk english the best I can, for Lady Daingerfield speacks nothing but high english, and the Colonel had his Education in England and is a verry smart Man.... I am obliged to continue with Coll. Daingerfield for four years if he insists on it, and for teaching his own Childreen I have Bed, Board, washing and all kind of Cloaths during the above time, and for what schoolars I can get more than his Childreen I have five shillings currancy per Quarter for each of them.... As to my living I eat at their own table.... Our Family consists of the Coll. His Lady & four Childreen a house-keeper an overseer and myself all white. But how many blacks young and old the Lord only knows for I believe there is about thirty that works every day in the field besides the servants about the house....

(continued on next page)

Summary:
I am living with Colonel William Dangerfield.... I teach his children to read, write, and work with numbers. His boys are 8, 6, and 4 years old, and he also has 1 daughter.... I must speak my best English because Lady Dangerfield speaks very educated English. For teaching the children for the next 4 years, I get a place to sleep and wash, food, and clothes. If I can teach more children, I will get 5 shillings for each one, every three months. I eat at the table with the family, a housekeeper, and the workers' super-visor. We are all white. There are about 30 black people here who work in the field and help in the house.

Vocabulary:
Board = free food
figure = work with numbers
high english = language of
   the well educated
obliged = required
overseer = workers' boss

Summary:

The clothes here are very white. They boil them before they wash them. If I want to, I can wear clean clothes every day. My school house is at the end of a street and is 20 feet long and 12 feet wide. I sleep there in a fine feather bed with cotton sheets, a blanket, and a bed spread…. So far, I have 10 students. One is deaf. He can write and work with numbers a little. He is 14 years old. His father pays me 10 shillings every three months. Another student is a young man, a wood worker, who studies with me every night and some Sundays. He pays me 40 shillings for the year. He is a carpenter, and earns 30 pounds a year, plus free bed and board.

Vocabulary:

Boyle = boil
bairn = child
Carpenter = wood worker
Deaff = deaf
Schollars = students

They wash here the whitest that ever I seed for they first Boyle all the Cloaths with soap, and then wash them, and I may put on my clean linen every day if I please. My school is a neate little House 20 foot Long and 12 foot wide and it stands by itself at the end of an Avenue…there comes a bonny black bairn every morning to clean it out and make my bed for I sleep in it by myself. I have a verry fine feather bed under me, and a pair of sheets, a thin fold of a Blanket and a Cotton bed spread is all my bed cloaths…. I have as yet only ten Schollars One of which is both Deaff and Dumb and his Father pays me ten shillings per Quarter for him…he can write mostly for any thing he wants and understand the value of every figure, and can work single addition a little. He is about fourteen years of age. Another of them is a young man a house Carpenter who Attends me every night with candle light and every Sunday that I don't go to Church for which he pays me fourty shillings a year. He is Carpenter for a gentlemen who lives two miles from me and has Thirty pound [currency] a year, free bedd and board.

Source: Alan Gallay, ed., *Voices of the Old South*. Athens, Georgia: The University of Georgia Press, 1994, p. 116.

Freedom of Faith

Many colonists came to America in search of a safe place to practice their religious beliefs. Puritans came to New England, Quakers settled in Pennsylvania, and Catholics, in Maryland. Some religious groups became very intolerant of outsiders, and created laws to punish those who held different beliefs. However, a few powerful leaders started colonies where people could truly be free.

Church and State—No Union upon Any Terms.

The debate over separation of church and state continued to be an issue, long after the Colonial period. This Thomas Nast cartoon shows the "state" turning all of the different religious groups away.

At first, settlers didn't separate their church from their government. Each colony built a meetinghouse, used for both worship and community business.

Some early meetinghouses were oddly decorated. Anyone who killed a wolf could collect a reward from the community. Many who did then hung the animal's head on the outside wall of the meeting house.

Rule by Church

...itans first arrived at Cape Cod in 1620. They came to
. being punished for their religious beliefs. However, once
...ierica, they set up rules that punished other people who did
their religion! The church joined with the state (the govern-
...ce people to obey these religious demands.

...otton, a Puritan minister (1584-1652), was a firm believer in
the u.. .n of church and state. He wanted to prevent non-believers (non-
Puritans) from holding public office or from having any position of power in
the church or the government. He said that only "saints" could be trusted to
be in power.

Summary:

Rule by God is the best type of government for a Christian community; free men should choose it.

A government made for the good of both church and state is the best.

A government that gives power only to the saints is the best for a Christian community.

Vocabulary:

administration = those in
   command
civil = public
commonwealth = community
provision = condition, terms
Theocracy = government
   in which God is thought
   to be the supreme ruler

Theocracy, or to make the Lord God our governor, is the best form of government in a Christian commonwealth, and...men who are free to choose...ought to establish [it]....

That form of government [in which] the best provision is made for the good both of the church and of the civil state is the best form of a government....

That form of government [in which] the power of civil administration is denied unto unbelievers and [is] committed to the saints is the best form of government in a Christian Commonwealth....

Source: John Cotton, "A Discourse About Civil Government." Found in *Church and State in American History.* Englewood, N.J.: D.C. Heath and Company, 1965, p. 7.

Challenging Church Rule

Roger Williams, an English Puritan minister, came to Massachusetts in 1631 and served as a teacher in the church. The Puritans asked him to leave the colony in 1635, because he disagreed with those in power about the need for religious freedom. He left, but remained in America. In 1636, he started the settlement of Providence, where religious freedom and democratic rule were practiced.

In 1644, Williams wrote about religious freedom and the need to separate the church from the state. His writing so angered the English government that it ordered the document to be publicly burned.

…the proper meanes whereby the Civill Power may and should attaine its end are only Politicall…

…the erecting and establishing what forme of Civill Government may seeme in wisedom most meet, according to general rules of the Word, and the state of the people.

…the making, publishing, and establishing of wholesome Civill Lawes, not only such as concerne Civill Justice, but also the free passage of true Religion.… And yet such Lawes, though conversant about Religion, may still be counted Civill Lawes, as on the contrary, an Oath doth still remaine Religious, though conversant about Civill matters.

Source: Roger Williams, *The Bloudy Tenent of Persecution for Cause of Conscience*. Found in Edmund S. Morgan, ed., *Puritan Political Ideas, 1558-1794*. Indianapolis: The Bobbs-Merrill Company, Inc., 1965, pp. 198-200. Originally published in London, 1644.

Summary:

…Only a political public government is proper…

…Set up public government in a way that most think is wise and in keeping with God's words and the people's needs.

…Public laws should promote justice and freedom of religion.… Public and religious laws may each make reference to the other, but should remain separate.

Vocabulary:

Civill (civil) = belonging to citizens; public

conversant = familiar with

erecting = making, constructing

establishing = setting up

Persecution = hurting

Politicall (political) = related to a government system

Tenent = view

Quakers in America

Quakers (members of the Religious Society of Friends) first arrived in the New World in 1655, and eventually went to Boston. Their religious beliefs were very different from those of the Puritans, and they soon learned that the New World Puritans would not accept them. Two Quaker women were imprisoned under suspicion of witchcraft.

The Puritans passed laws against Quakerism, and when more Quakers arrived, they were severely punished. The Quakers discovered that the only safe place for them in America was in Providence, Roger Williams' settlement. *(See cover illustration of the Narragansett Indians welcoming Williams.)*

William Penn made an arrangement with the king of England for the land that would one day be called Pennsylvania. Even though England considered Penn the landowner, he paid the Indians for this same land as a sign of respect. He believed the Quakers could create a nearly perfect society in their new settlement.

The Landing of William Penn, *by Thomas Birch. William Penn, founder of Philadelphia, became a Quaker while he still lived in England. When he came to America, he befriended the Indians and set up a Quaker colony in 1681.* (Courtesy of the Museum of Fine Arts, Boston)

Living by Conscience

William Penn's *Liberty of Conscience* was written for Quakers who were being punished for their beliefs while living in England. It also served as a guide for Quakers newly settled in Pennsylvania. In this work he explained his beliefs about the need for freedom of thought.

…If we allow the honour of our creation due to God only, and that no other besides himself has endowed us with those excellent gifts of Understanding, Reason, Judgment, and Faith, and consequently that he only is the object, as well as the author, both of our faith, Worship, and Service; then whosoever shall interpose their authority to enact faith and worship in a way that seems not to us congruous with what he has discovered to us to be faith and worship…or to restrain us from what we are persuaded is our indispensable duty, they evidently usurp this authority, and invade his incommunicable right of government over conscience.…

Source: Frederick B. Tolles and E. Gordon Alderfer, eds., *The Witness of William Penn*. New York: The Macmillan Company, 1959, pp. 69-71. Originally published as *The Great Case for Liberty of Conscience Once More Briefly Debated and Defended*. Newgate, 1670.

Summary:
Only God could have given us the gifts of intelligence and common sense. He also gave us the skills to make good decisions and to have faith. Therefore, He is the only one we can worship and serve. Anyone who gets in the way of this worship is taking away God's right to rule our thoughts.

Vocabulary

congruous = proper; fitting
conscience = sense of
   right and wrong
enact = make into law
endowed = given
incommunicable = unable
   to be communicated
indispensable = needed
interpose = put in
restrain = restrict
usurp = seize; grab

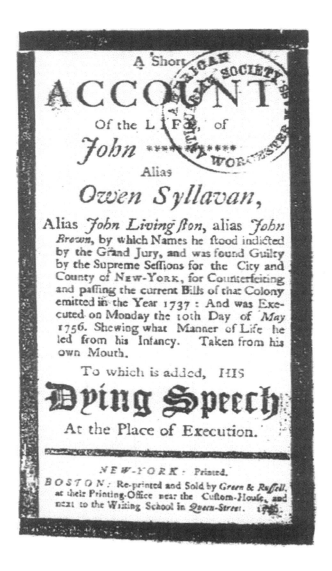

A Short ACCOUNT Of the LIFE, of John ********
Alias
Owen Syllavan,
Alias *John Livingston*, alias *John Brown*, by which Names he stood indicted by the Grand Jury, and was found Guilty by the Supreme Sessions for the City and County of NEW-YORK, for Counterfeiting and passing the current Bills of that Colony emitted in the Year 1737 : And was Executed on Monday the 10th Day of *May* 1756. Shewing what Manner of Life he led from his Infancy. Taken from his own Mouth.

To which is added, HIS

𝕯𝖞𝖎𝖓𝖌 𝕾𝖕𝖊𝖊𝖈𝖍

At the Place of Execution.

NEW-YORK · Printed.
BOSTON: Re-printed and Sold by *Green & Russell*, at their Printing-Office near the Custom-House, and next to the Writing School in *Queen-Street*. 17...

Confessions

Starting about 1699, statements by criminals about to be put to death were published. It was hoped that the stories would improve the behavior of other citizens. For example, Owen Syllavan admitted that even before he was 11 years old, "I was always in all kinds of Mischief; so that I never minded Father nor Mother, Sister nor Brother; but went on in all Manner of Vice." Confessions such as Owen's became popular reading.

Source: Daniel E. Williams, ed. *Pillars of Salt: An Anthology of Early American Criminal Narratives.* Madison, Wisconsin: Madison House, 1993, pp. 142-3.

Making and Breaking Laws

The New World communities had to make rules to live by. At first the colonists based their laws loosely on those in England. They also made laws to enforce their religious beliefs. Some of the colonial laws and some of the punishments might seem strange to us today.

Dress Rules

At first, Puritans were very strict about what everyone wore. However, as some Puritans became richer, the community had a hard time enforcing the dress rules. Instead of trying to control everyone's appearance, the courts decided that what anyone could wear depended on social class. Town watchmen made sure that no one dressed beyond his or her proper place in life.

We declare our utter detestation and dislike that men and women of mean condition, education and callings should take upon themselves the garb of gentlemen by the wearing of gold or silver lace, or buttons, or…to walk in great boots; or women to wear silk…, which, though allowable to persons of greater estates, or more liberal education, yet we cannot but judge it intolerable in persons of such like condition.

Source: Gustavus Myers, *Ye Olden Blue Laws,* New York: The Century Co., 1921, p. 38.

Summary:
It disgusts us that poor men and women with little education and low jobs dress like gentlemen, or that those women wear silk. Such fine things are acceptable for richer or better educated people, but not for people like that.

Vocabulary
callings = jobs
condition = rank
detestation = disgust
estates = wealth
garb = clothes
intolerable = unbearable
liberal = tolerant, open-minded
mean condition = low rank
utter = complete

Laws against Appearance of Sin

For such things as working in their gardens on Sunday, the Puritans punished their citizens with fines, whipping, and branding. In 1674, they passed a law against the appearance of sin.

Summary:

It is the duty of this Court to prevent the appearance of sin and wickedness. From now on, no single woman or wife whose husband is away may entertain or rent rooms to any guest that the town officials dislike. On conviction, the penalty is £15 [in English money £=pound] per week, or physical punishment. Whipping shall not be more than ten lashes. All police officers are to keep watch for such cases.

Vocabulary:

accounting = considering
cognizance = knowledge
commissioners = authorities
conviction = being found
   guilty
corporally = bodily
due means = proper ways
henceforth = from now on
inmate = tenant
magistrate = judge
selectmen = town officials
sojourner = boarder
thereof = of it

This Court, accounting it their duty by all due means to prevent appearance of sin and wickedness of any kind, do order that henceforth it shall not be lawful for any single woman or wife in the absence of her husband to entertain or lodge any inmate or sojourner with the dislike of the selectmen of the town, or magistrate, or commissioners who may have cognizance thereof, upon penalty of £15 per week, on conviction thereof before any court or magistrate, or be corporally punished, not exceeding ten stripes; and all constables are to take cognizance hereof for information of such cases.

Source: Gustavus Myers, *Ye Olden Blue Laws,* New York: The Century Co., 1921, pp. 116-7.

Laws about Religious Beliefs

The English were Protestants, and many colonies did not welcome people of different beliefs. Maryland was open to Roman Catholics, although they could not hold public office. Any people who denied basic Christian beliefs would lose their Maryland property.

To the Puritans in Massachusetts, any religion different from their own was sinful—and illegal. In 1647, the Massachusetts Colony passed laws forbidding Roman Catholic priests or missionaries from entering their territory. The Puritans were especially hard on Quakers, another group that had come to the New World in search of religious freedom.

…If any Quaker or Quakers shall presume…to come into this jurisdiction, every such male Quaker shall for the first offense have one of his ears cut off, and be kept at work in the house of correction till he can be sent away…and for the second offense shall have his other ear cut off…. Every woman Quaker presuming, etc., shall be severely whipped, and kept at the house of correction at work until she shall be sent away…. If she comes again she is to be like used. And for every Quaker he or she that shall a third time herein again offend, they shall have their tongues bored through with a hot iron….

Source: Gustavus Myers, *Ye Olden Blue Laws,* New York: The Century Co., 1921, pp. 249-50.

Summary:

If any Quaker dares to enter this territory—the first time, every male will have one of his ears cut off and will work in jail. The second time, his other ear will be cut off. Every Quaker woman will be severely whipped and will work in jail. If she returns, she will be treated the same. The third time, every male or female Quaker will have their tongues bored through with a hot iron.

Vocabulary:
presume = dare
jurisdiction = territory
like used = treated the
   same
herein = in this

Witchcraft trial, based on a painting by Howard Pyle. (Courtesy of the *Granger Collection*, the Bettman Archive)

Convicting Witches

During the seventeenth century, most people believed in witches. It was thought that a witch served Satan and spread evil among humans. In the New England colonies, the sudden death of a farm animal or the illness of a child could make people suspect that a witch was at work. Many accused "witches" were put to death in Salem Village, Massachusetts, in 1692.

People were found guilty of witchcraft just because someone else claimed to have been hurt by them—sometimes in a dream. The accused were often tortured or severely "tested" until they confessed. Sometimes family members, including children, were forced to confess that a parent was a witch. The youngest found guilty of witchcraft was four years old.

A personal statement was made by seven women arrested as witches at Andover, Massachusetts, in 1692.

…we knowing ourselves altogether Innocent of that Crime, we were all exceedingly astonished and amazed, and consternated and affrighted even out of our Reason; and our nearest and dearest Relations, seeing us in that dreadful condition, and knowing our great danger, apprehending there was no other way to save our lives…but by confessing our selves…indeed that Confession that is said we made, was no other than what was suggested to us by some Gentlemen; they telling us, that we were Witches, and they knew it, and we knew it, and they knew that we knew it, which made us think that it was so; and our understanding, our reason, and our faculties almost gone, we were not capable of judging our condition; as also the hard measures they used with us, rendred us uncapable of making our Defence; but said anything and everything which they desired, and most of what we said, was but in effect a consenting to what they said. Sometime after when we were better composed, they telling of us what we had confessed, we did profess that we were Innocent.…

Source: Lt. Gov. Thomas Hutchinson, *The History of the Province of Massachusetts Bay from the Charter of King William & Mary in 1691 Until the Year 1750*, Harvard College/Kraus; Reprint, 1936, Chapter I.

Summary:
We knew we were innocent. We were all surprised and frightened. Our relatives understood that there was no other way to save our lives. Our confession was suggested by some gentlemen who said we were witches. They made us believe it. We weren't capable of making a decision. After the hard time they gave us, we said anything they wanted. Most of it was just agreeing with what they said. Later, when we were calm, they told us what we had confessed. We said we were innocent.

Vocabulary:
affrighted = frightened
altogether = completely
apprehending = understanding
better composed = calmer
consenting = agreement
consternated = confused
exceedingly = very
faculties = abilities
profess = say
reason = intelligence
rendred (rendered) = made
uncapable = unable

A notice of a slave auction from about 1763. (Courtesy of the Library of Congress Collection)

Human Property

During the colonial period and beyond, some people thought of other people as property to be bought and sold. Like others of their time, the American colonists wanted servants over whom they had complete control. The colonists captured and enslaved some Native Americans, but Indians often escaped and returned to their homes. Africans brought to the colonies by ship were in an unfamiliar land with no means of escape unless aided by sympathetic colonists.

Punishments were much more harsh for slaves than for people who were free. Of course, helping a slave escape was a crime for which anyone could be punished.

Colonial Punishments

In Mark Twain's novel, *The Adventures of Huckleberry Finn,* Huck and his friend Tom Sawyer watch the treatment of two criminals. The men are thieves and con-men, and surely deserve some punishment. But after seeing them tarred and feathered, Huck comments that "Human beings *can* be awful cruel to one another."

In the seventeenth and eighteenth centuries, punishment for criminals was often more violent than the crime itself. Many punishments used by the colonists might seem awfully cruel to us now. Other methods might just seem odd.

All of the colonies required their towns and villages to be ready to deal with criminals. In Virginia, certain equipment for administering punishments was considered necessary, as *The 1662 Statute Books of Virginia* describes.

The court in every county shall cause to be set up near a Court House a Pillory, a pair of Stocks, a Whipping Post and a Ducking-Stool in such place as they think convenient, which not being set up within six month after the date of this act the said Court shall be fined 5,000 lbs. of tobacco.

Source: Alice Morse Earle, *Curious Punishments of Bygone Days,* New York: Macmillan, 1896, p. 18.

Summary:
The court of every county must set up a pillory, a pair of stocks, a whipping post, and a ducking stool in a convenient place near the courthouse. If these are not set up within six months of this order, that court will be fined 5,000 pounds of tobacco.

Vocabulary:
act = order
said = named before

The Pillory

In Colonial America, criminals were often put on public display. The pillory held them in place while other people looked at them, made comments, and sometimes threw rotten vegetables. Stocks were similar to the pillory, but they held the legs of criminals who were seated. Sometimes the punishment was much worse than just being on view.

Whipping

Whipping was a favorite punishment in Colonial America. People were whipped for being drunk, stealing, and even for gossiping. Colonial school-children who misbehaved were whipped with small branches.

Whipping posts were put up in every village and town. The criminal was tied to the post, stripped to the waist, and whipped so that everyone could watch.

However, not just every kind of person was whipped. Boston laws said that no "true gentleman or any man equall to a gentlemen shall be punished with whipping unless his crime be very shameful."

A Bostonian named Samuel Breck recalled an eighteenth-century whipping post he had seen as a child.

Summary:

The whipping post was in a main street, near a writing school. Students saw punishments that would harden their hearts. Women were brought in a cage, tied to the post, and given 30 or 40 lashes on their bare backs. The prisoner screamed and the mob shouted.

Vocabulary:

bestowed = given
brutalize = make cruel
conspicuously = easily
    seen
culprit = lawbreaker
frequented = often visited
indulged = allowed
prominently = visibly
spectacle = sight

The large whipping-post painted red stood conspicuously and prominently in the most public street in the town. It was placed in State Street directly under the windows of a great writing school which I frequented, and from there the scholars were indulged in the spectacle of all kinds of punishment suited to harden their hearts and brutalize their feelings. Here women were taken in a huge cage in which they were dragged on wheels from prison, and tied to the post with bare backs on which thirty or forty lashes were bestowed among the screams of the culprit and the uproar of the mob.

Source: Alice Morse Earle, *Curious Punishments of Bygone Days,* New York: Macmillan, 1896, p. 81.

Gagging and Ducking

Some punishments were especially for people who complained too much—called scolds. In England and in the colonies, a metal gag was used, usually on women. Another type of gag was the cleft stick, which was also used on men.

Scolds were also ducked into a pond or river. Special seats were built to lower the person into the water and hold him or her there.

Ducking was also a punishment for slander (making false statements about another person).

The Records of the Massachusetts Bay Colony

6 September, Boston, 1636. Robert Shorthouse for swearinge by the bloud of God was sentenced to have his tongue put into a cleft stick, and soe stand for halfe an houre & Elizabeth wife of Thomas Applegate was censured to stand with her tongue in a cleft stick for half an houre for swearinge....

Source: Alice Morse Earle, *Curious Punishments of Bygone Days,* New York: Macmillan, 1896, p. 104.

Summary:
For swearing, Robert Shorthouse and Elizabeth each stood with their tongues in a cleft stick for half an hour.

Vocabulary:
bloud = blood
censured = condemned
halfe = half
houre = hour
soe = so
swearinge = swearing

The 1662 Statute Books of Virginia

In actions of slander caused by a man's wife, after judgment past for damages, the woman shall be punished by Ducking, and if the slander be such as the damages shall be adjudged as above 500 lbs. of Tobacco, then the woman shall have ducking for every 500 lbs. of Tobacco adjudged against the husband if he refuse to pay the Tobacco.

Source: Alice Morse Earle, *Curious Punishments of Bygone Days.* New York: Macmillan, 1896, p. 18.

Summary:
If a man's wife slanders, she will be punished by ducking. If the husband refuses to pay damages, she will be ducked again for every 500 lbs. of tobacco he owes.

Vocabulary:
adjudged = judged
slander = lying about a person

Tarring and Feathering

Boston customs official being tarred and feathered in 1774. (Courtesy of the Harvard College Library)

A letter from a loyal English subject in Boston during 1774 presents a vivid account of the cruelty of tarring and feathering.

Summary:

A poor man was stripped naked, then tarred and feathered. His arm was dislocated. People watched and some beat him. This horrible show went on for five hours.

Vocabulary:

cloaths = clothes
dislocated = pulled out of
    joint
exercised = done
featherd = feathered
Spectacle = show
sportive = playful
stript = stripped

The most shocking cruelty was exercised a few Nights ago, upon a poor Man…[he was] Tarrd, & featherd…. he was stript Stark naked, one of the severest cold nights this Winter, his body coverd all over with Tar, then with feathers, his arm dislocated in tearing off his cloaths, he was draggd in a Cart with thousands attending, some beating him with clubs & Knocking him out of the Cart, then in again. They gave him several severe whipings, at different parts of the Town. This Spectacle of horror & sportive cruelty was exhibited for about five hours.

Source: Ann Hulton, *Letters of a Loyalist Lady 1767–1776.* Cambridge: Harvard University Press, 1927.

What If You Got Sick?

The colonists suffered from many illnesses when they first settled in America. The water they drank was often impure because they had no sewage systems. Mosquitoes infected them with malaria. Before public dumps were provided, garbage and dead animals lay in the streets. Smallpox, which sometimes caused death, was common. Open wounds often became infected because of the lack of medicines. Many women and babies died during childbirth.

Doctors in colonial America had no training. They knew nothing about hygiene, how the human body worked, sanitation, or drugs. The first medical school in America did not open until the 1750s.

Native Americans and European Diseases

Most historians agree that death from European diseases was the main reason for the defeat of the Indians by the settlers. These Native Americans had no resistance to the illnessess colonists brought to this country. Many Indians died from smallpox. They also felt beaten because they saw their families and friends dying of diseases that didn't seem to bother the white people. They feared that God was on the side of the settlers.

William Bradford recalled the conditions of the Native Americans.

This spring, also, those Indians that lived about their trading house there fell sick of the small pox, and died most miserably; for a sorer disease cannot befall them; they fear it more than the plague; for usually they that have this disease have them in abundance, and for want of bedding and lining and other helps, they fall into a lamentable condition, as they lie on their hard mats....

(continued on next page)

Summary:

This spring, many Indians got small pox and died. They are afraid of the disease, for many of them catch it. Without clean bedding or other help, they get very sick.

Vocabulary:
abundance = plenty
lamentable = heartbreaking
plague = an infectious
   disease
small pox = an infectious
   disease
sorer = worse

Summary:

They die like a rotting animal in the cold: hurting and feverish. So many of them are ill, they can't help each other. They cannot build a fire, bring in drinking water, or even bury their dead. Many of the colonists feel sorry for them. They hear their pitiful cries. They bring them water, food, and wood, and build fires for them. And they bury them when they die. Chief Sachem has died, along with most of his family and friends. Thanks to God, none of the colonists got sick, even though they were with the Indians for many weeks.

Vocabulary:

compassion = caring
distempers = infections
fetch = get
hazard = danger
kindred = family
providence = guidance
tainted = infected
victuals = food

…and then being very sore, what with cold and other distempers, they die like rotten sheep. The condition of this people was so lamentable, and they fell down so generally of this disease, as they were (in the end) not able to help one another; no, not to make a fire, nor to fetch a little water to drink, nor any to bury the dead…. But those of the English house, (though at first they were afraid of the infection,) yet seeing their woeful and sad condition, and hearing their pitiful cries and lamentations, they had compassion of them, and daily fetched them wood and water, and made them fires, got them victuals whilst they lived, and buried them when they died. For very few of them escaped, notwithstanding they did what they could for them, to the hazard of themselves. The chief Sachem himself now died, and almost all his friends and kindred. But by the marvelous goodness and providence of God not one of the English was so much as sick, or in the least measure tainted with this disease, though they daily did these offices for them many weeks together.

Source: William Bradford, *Of Plymouth Plantation,* New York, Alfred A. Knopf, 1966.

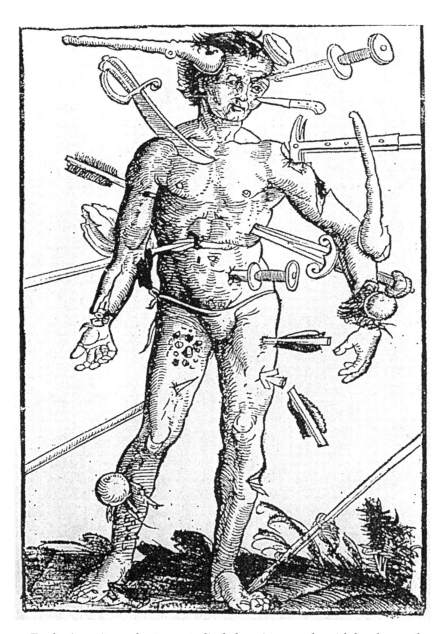

Early American doctors studied drawings and guidebooks made by European doctors. They even used other pictures drawn by early Romans and Greeks. This drawing of a "Wounded Man" showed where the human body might receive wounds during combat. This picture was first seen in a German medical magazine in 1517. It was used for over 300 years by military doctors. (Artist unknown, courtesy of the National Archives.)

Untrained Doctors

Europeans often made fun of the American colonists' crude ways of living. Dr. Alexander Hamilton, an English physician, traveled from Maryland up to Maine in 1744. He found much to mock, as he watched our country's early doctors trying to practice medicine.

Summary:

We had just sat down when some town leaders came in. They probably wanted to know who the strangers were. With them was a man wearing a wool cap. He had huge blackened hands. They said he used to be a shoemaker. He became a doctor after curing an old woman of a bad disease. After that, many people asked him for medical help. He could make more money as a doctor, so he decided to fix people instead of shoes.

Vocabulary:

awls (awl) = drill; pick
band = group
cobbling = fixing
gallipots = turpentine,
   from pine trees
mortal = deadly
pestilent = contagious
physic = medicine
styled = called
worsted = wool

…We had no sooner sat down when there came in a band of the town politicians in short jackets and trousers, being probably curious to know who them strangers were who had newly arrived in town. Among the rest was a fellow with a worsted cap and great black fists. They styled him a doctor. Flat told me he had been a shoemaker in town and was a notable fellow at his trade, but happening two years ago to cure an old woman of a pestilent mortal disease, he thereby acquired the character of a physician, was applied to from all quarters, and finding the practice of physic a more profitable business than cobbling, he laid aside his awls and leather, got himself some gallipots, and instead of cobbling of soles, fell to cobbling of human bodies.…

Source: Alexander Hamilton, *Gentleman's Progress: The Itinerarium of Dr. Alexander Hamilton.* Chapel Hill: University of North Carolina Press, 1948.

Dentistry

Throughout most of history, having teeth worked on was a painful process. Teeth were often pulled because of decay. There was no numbing medicine. Toothbrushes hadn't been invented yet. Salt water rubbed on the teeth with a cloth was the only way to clean teeth. Dr. Alexander Hamilton continues with his findings.

I supped upon fry'd chicken and bacon, and after supper the conversation turned upon politics, news, and the dreaded French war; but it was so very lumpish and heavy that it disposed me mightily to sleep. This learned company consisted of the landlord, his overseer and miller, and another greasy thumb'd fellow who, as I understood, professed physic and particularly surgery. In the drawing of teeth, he practiced upon the housemaid, a dirty piece of lumber, who made such screaming and squalling as made me imagine there was murder going forwards in the house. However, the artist got the tooth out at last with a great clumsy pair of blacksmith's forceps; and indeed it seemed to require such an instrument, for when he showed it to us, it resembled a horsenail more than a tooth....

Source: Alexander Hamilton, *Gentleman's Progress: The Itinerarium of Dr. Alexander Hamilton.* Chapel Hill: University of North Carolina Press, 1948.

Summary:
After supper, we talked about government, news, and the French war. I found the talk dull, and it made me sleepy. I was talking with the owner of the land and his head worker. Another man with dirty hands sat with us. He said he was a doctor who mostly did surgery. He pulled a tooth from a worthless housekeeper for practice. Her screams were so loud, it sounded as though someone was being killed. He used a huge pair of pliers that belonged to the black-smith. When the tooth finally came out, we saw it. It looked more like a huge horseshoe nail than a tooth.

Vocabulary:
disposed = caused
lumpish = crude
miller = flour factory worker
overseer = head worker
squalling = squawk
supped = ate

Home Remedies

Some colonists used plants as medicines to cure illnesses. Europeans and people around the world had been using them for centuries. The roots or leaves were often dried and powdered before being mixed with water to drink. Settlers found some of the same plants in America they had used in Europe.

The Indians also used herbs (dried plants), roots, and barks. They taught the settlers about new plants that worked as cures for sicknesses.

Some of these cures really worked, and others either had no effect or made people sick. As the years passed, the colonists became more skilled at picking the good plants.

Summary:
Take a piece of salt beef and roast it in hot ashes, then clean it and put it on the wound. The bleeding will stop.

Vocabulary:
Cleane = clean
hott = hot
imediatly = immediately
peec = piece
Rost = roast

To Stench Bleeding in a Wound

Take a peec of Salt Beef & Rost it in the hott Ashes then make it Cleane & put it into the wound & the blood will stop imediatly

Source: Dr. Zerobabel Endecott, found in George Francis Dow, *Everyday Life in the Massachusetts Bay Colony,* New York: Dover Books, 1988, pp.180-1

Summary:
Take rye flour and make a paste and roll it thin. Make a pie with it filled with sage and rosemary leaves. Bake until dry then beat it up and take 1/2 spoonful at a time in a cup of beer.

Vocabulary:
greene = green
past = paste
Rie flower = rye flour
Role = roll

An other

Take Rie flower make past with water Role it thin and with ye greene Leaues of Sage & a Littl Rosemary fill it as pye bake it very dry beat altogether & take halfe a spoonefull at a time in a wine Cupfull of your beere

Source: Dr. Zerobabel Endecott, found in George Francis Dow, *Everyday Life in the Massachusetts Bay Colony,* New York: Dover Books, 1988, pp. 186-7.

Afterword: Changes

In 1741, Benjamin Franklin started a new magazine in Philadelphia. Before then, colonial magazines had reprinted papers from English journals. But many selections in Franklin's *The General Magazine and Historical Chronicle for all the British Plantations in America* were written by colonists. Included were poems and papers from Virginia, Massachusetts, New York, Pennsylvania, and South Carolina. It even reviewed books published in the colonies. Franklin also wrote about the colonies.

The first drudgery of settling new colonies, which confines the attention of people to mere necessities, is now pretty well over; and there are many in every province in circumstances, that set them at ease, and afford leisure to cultivate the finer arts, and improve the common stock of knowledge....

Source: Benjamin Franklin, "A Proposal for Promoting Useful Knowledge among the British Plantations in America" (Philadelphia, 1743). Found in James Truslow Adams, *Provincial Society: 1690-1763. A History of American Life, Volume III*. Chicago: Quadrangle Books, 1971. The Macmillan Company, 1927, p. ix.

Summary:
At first, the hard work made colonists give all their attention to daily needs. Now, in every colony, people have more time to encourage the fine arts and improve the community's knowledge.

Vocabulary:
drudgery = hard labor
confines = limits
mere = simple
province = colony
circumstances = conditions
afford = provide
leisure = free time
cultivate = encourage

People born in the colonies were becoming scientists and writers. Artists and craftsmen, such as furniture makers, were inventing new American styles. The colonists were developing an American identity.

Research Activities/Things to Do

- William Bradford's descriptions of life at the Plymouth Plantation [actually referred to as Plimoth Plantation in most early documents] are very helpful to historians and students. Keep an accurate journal of one full day in your life that might be of interest to future historians studying the beginning of the 21st century.

- Most of the earliest colonists came to America in search of religious freedom. Why then, do you think, they were often so intolerant of members of other religious groups?

- In 1649 the Toleration Act provided a safer haven for Catholics in the Maryland colony. Pretend the year is 1650. Acting as the governor of your own new colony, create a religious freedom proposal to accept and respect the religious beliefs of those who may live in your colony. Are women, slaves, and Indians included?

- Colonial devices such as stocks, pillories, and ducking stools tended to publicly humiliate the offenders as much as punish them. Do you believe these methods were effective in reducing crime? Why or why not?

- Following are some popular names from the Colonial period in America:
  Comfort, Deliverance, Peace, Hope, Patience, Charity,
  Faith, Love, Joy, and Rejoice.

  How do they reflect colonial society? What are some popular names now that reflect different ethnic groups? popular leaders? entertainers?

- By the mid-1700s, American English included many new words, some of which came from various European languages. Other words were borrowed from the Native Americans, such as squash, canoe, raccoon, and skunk. Why were words like these added to the English language? What new words can you think of that have been added recently?

- Do some research on your own to find out how women were treated compared to men in the Colonial period. Look into areas of education, property rights, work opportunities, etc.

Written Document

In September of 1635, a booklet was published in England to report on life in Maryland. Following are a few excerpts from Chapter V of the booklet describing the author's opinions and observations of the local Indians. After reading the excerpts, use the document worksheet to evaluate the document.

A Relation of Maryland

Experience has taught us that, when treated with kindness and fairness, the Natives are not only peaceful, but friendly, and have upon occasions performed like any good neighbor or friend in the most Civil parts of Christendom . . . .

These Natives live like it was when the world was under the Law of Nature. All men are free but are yet subject to command for the public defense. . . .

The women serve their husbands, make bread, and dress their meat, such as they kill in hunting, or get by fishing. The women also make Mats, which serve to cover their houses, and for beds. Also they make baskets which are very handsome.

In their wars and hunting, they use Bows and Arrows. The Arrow-heads are made of Flint-stone, the top of a Deer's horn, or some Fish bone, which they fasten with a sort of glue that they make. They also use in wars a short club which they call a Tomahawk . . . .

It is never heard of that those of a Nation will steal from another, and the English trust them to transport goods and deliver letters. Their conversation with each other is peaceful and free from all gossip. They are very hospitable to their own people and to strangers . . . .

I therefore conclude that, since God Almighty has made this Country so large and fruitful and that the people are such you have heard described, it is much more Prudent and Charitable to Civilize and Christianize these people than to Kill them, Rob them, and Hunt them down from place to place, as you would a wolf.

Written Document Worksheet

Based on Worksheet from *Teaching with Documents,*
National Archives and Records Administration

1. **Type of document:**

   ❏ Newspaper   ❏ Diary   ❏ Advertisement

   ❏ Letter   ❏ Ship Manifest   ❏ Deed

   ❏ Memo   ❏ Journal   ❏ Other_____

2. **Unique Characteristics of the Document:**

   ❏ Interesting Stationery   ❏ "RECEIVED" stamp   ❏ Unusual Fold Marks

   ❏ Handwritten   ❏ "CLASSIFIED" stamp   ❏ Written notations

   ❏ Official Seal   ❏ Other stamp_____   ❏ Other_____

3. **Date(s) of Document:**   ❏ No Date

4. **Author of Document:**   **Position:**

5. **For what audience was the document written?**

6. **Key Information** *(In your opinion, what are the 3 most important points of the document?)*

   a.

   b.

   c.

7. **Why do you think the document was written?**

8. **Choose a quote from the document that helped you to know why it was written:**

9. **Write down two clues which you got from the document that tell you something about life in the U.S. at the time the document was written:**

10. **Write a question to the author that you feel is unanswered in the document:**

11. **What do you think the response to the document was?**

Sample Graphic

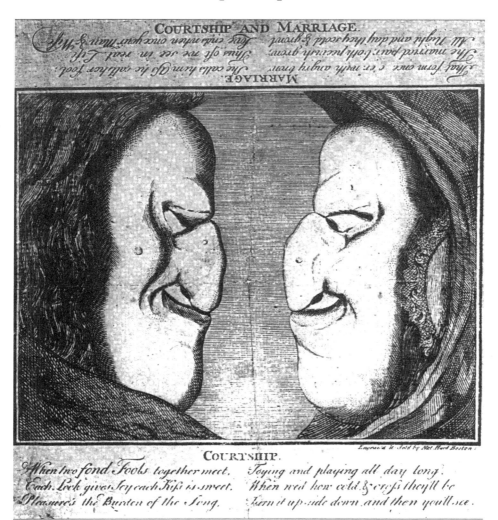

- Using the Analyzing Graphics Worksheet on the next page, analyze this Colonial picture puzzle on courtship and marriage. Make sure you turn the picture upside down in your study.

- Interpret the cartoon found on page 23 using the Graphics Worksheet.

- Find several different prints of the paintings by Edward Hicks, all entitled "Peacable Kingdom." How do they differ from each other? How are they alike? (Note: Many art books and internet sites have copies.)

Analyzing Graphics, Cartoons, and Photos Worksheet

Some or all of the following will help you to analyze an historic photo, cartoon, or other type of graphic. Use the worksheet to jot down notes about the piece being evaluated.

1. **What is the subject matter?**

2. **What details provide clues?**
   - ❏ scene
   - ❏ buildings
   - ❏ people
   - ❏ clothing
   - ❏ artifacts
   - ❏ time of day
   - ❏ style of graphic
   - ❏ written message
   - ❏ season
   - ❏ B&W/color

3. **Can you determine the location?   The intended audience?**

4. **What is the date? If there is no date, can you guess the period?**

5. **What is the purpose of the poster, ad, artwork, photo, etc.?**
   - ❏ private use
   - ❏ recording an event
   - ❏ propaganda
   - ❏ art
   - ❏ advertising
   - ❏ Other_____

6. **Describe the tone (mood) of the picture?**

7. **Are there clues which tell you if the creator was sympathetic to the topic or cause?**

8. **Can you tell anything about the point of view of the graphic?**
   - ❏ social
   - ❏ political
   - ❏ educational
   - ❏ recreational
   - ❏ sales tool

9. **What details make this piece effective or ineffective?**

10. **Explain the message in your own words.**

11. **Are any symbols used in the graphic? Are they verbal or visual? Describe what each symbol represents.**

    <u>Object</u>   <u>Symbolizes</u>

Sample Painting

William Penn traded goods for Indian lands in 1682. (Courtesy of the Thomas Gilcrease Institute of American History and Art)

• Analyze this painting, using the worksheet on the opposite page.

• Write a short story or poem about the scene pictured here.

_____

_____

_____

_____

_____

_____

_____

_____

_____

Differences between the Colonies

by

Jeanne Munn Bracken

The following summarizes several major differences between the northern and southern colonies, in broad terms, and recognizing that exceptions exist:

Source: Adapted from "The Stage Was Set," by Jeanne Munn Bracken, *Life in the Southern Colonies:Jamestown, Williamsburg, St. Mary's City and Beyond,* Discovery Enterprises, Ltd., 1997. pp. 62-3.

- ◆ The northern colonies were settled by religious dissenters determined to carve a home in the wilderness, where they could worship freely. The southern colonies were settled by hirelings and adventurers determined to wrest the wealth of furs, precious metals, and other natural resources from the wilderness.

- ◆ The northern colonists were highly religious, with the settlers judged by their adherence to local church customs, exhibiting intolerance to those with different beliefs. In the southern colonies, the church played a weaker role in the lives of the settlers, opening the way for more religious tolerance for those with varying views.

- ◆ The northern climate was characterized by harsh winters and a short growing season, with crops primarily grown for local sustenance. This fostered the development of fishing, lumbering, and eventually (after the Industrial Revolution) manufacturing industries. The southern climate featured inhospitable summers, but a long growing season, leading to exportable crops such as rice, indigo, cotton, and tobacco.

- ◆ Work for those in the early northern colonies included family farms and the craftsmen and artisans whose products supported them. Work in the southern colonies required a very large laboring class of servants, which led to the slave system.

- ◆ In the North, seaports developed around shipbuilding and cargo centers. Southerners used foreign-built ships that sailed directly to local wharves.

◆ The North saw cities like New York, Philadelphia, and Boston grow and thrive as centers of culture and industry, with a variety of shops and well-respected schools. The southern population was both more isolated (in scattered farms and plantations—with few towns and fewer cities) and more concentrated (with plantations forming towns and families of their own, providing virtually all of the inhabitants' needs).

◆ The northern colonies grew with working and merchant classes. The South had a small wealthy class, a growing class of former indentured servants who had earned their freedom, and a huge laboring underclass— with few or no rights or property.

◆ The northern colonies generally adopted a fiercely independent political structure that was more likely to oppose royalty and absentee government. The South, with its chartered royal colonies, retained a political and social structure more likely to favor the king and his representatives.

The stage was set well before the American Revolution for the clash that was to follow nearly a century later in the Civil War, still known today — south of the Mason-Dixon Line—as 'The War between the States.'

• In your research, find concrete examples of the statements made in this essay.

• Add to Mrs. Bracken's essay other differences between the northern and southern colonies which you have observed in your studies.

53

Suggested Further Reading

The books listed below are suggested readings in American literature, which tie in with the *Researching American History Series*. The selections were made based on feedback from teachers and librarians currently using them in interdisciplinary classes for students in grades 5 to 12. Those books with a double asterisk (**) are particularly recommended. Of course there are many other historical novels that would be appropriate to tie in with the titles in this series.

Life in the American Colonies

    * *The Scarlet Letter*, Nathaniel Hawthorne - HS

    * *Calico Bush*, Rachel Field - M

  ** *Pocahontas and the Strangers*, Clyde Robert Bulla - EL

    * *Pocahontas: Powaton Peacemaker*, Anne Holler - M (biography)

    * *The Sign of the Beaver*, Elizabeth George Speare - M

    * *Saturnalia*, Paul Fleischman - M

The Pilgrims

    * *Constance: A Story of Early Plymouth*, Patricia Clapp - M

    * *Cape Cod*, William Martin - HS

    * *Stranded at Plimoth Plantation 1626*, Gary Brown - M (fictional diary)

    * *Williamsburg Household*, Joan Anderson - EL/M

The Salem Witch Trials

    * *The Crucible*, Arthur Miller - HS (play)

    * *Witch of Blackbird Pond*, Elizabeth George Speare - M

    * *Tituba of Salem Village*, Ann Petry - EL/M

    * *Break with Charity*, Rinaldi - M

Colonial America

The following titles in the *Perspectives on History Series* from Discovery Enterprises, Ltd., include primary and secondary sources about life in the American colonies. Those with an asterisk(*) also cover the subject as it relates to other periods in American History.

*American Quakers**

*Architecture: An Image for America**

Colonial Triangular Trade: An Economy Based on Human Misery

The Constitution and the Bill of Rights

*Crime and Punishment: The Colonial Period to the New Frontier**

Cry "Witch": The Salem Witch Trials - 1692

The Declaration of Independence

Faith Unfurled: The Pilgrims' Quest for Freedom

The French and Indian War: Prelude to American Independence

*Indians of the Northeast**

Life in the American Colonies: Daily Lifestyles of the Early Settlers

Life in the Southern Colonies: Jamestown, Williamsburg, St. Mary's City and Beyond

*Making a Statement with Song: Songs Reflecting the Social, Economic and Political Climate in American History**

*Presidential Elections: 1789-1996**

*The Shakers**

The Shot Heard 'Round the World: The Beginnings of the American Revolution

*The Struggle for Religious Freedom in America**

Women in the American Revolution

For information on these and other titles from Discovery Enterprises, Ltd., call or write to: Discovery Enterprises, Ltd., 31 Laurelwood Drive, Carlisle, MA 01741 Phone: 978-287-5401 Fax: 978-287-5402